The *Chloe* Chronicles

The  Chronicles
Life Lessons I Learned From My Cocker Spaniel

Judi Mason

DIVA Ink Publishers
Atlanta, Georgia

The Chloe Chronicles
Copyright © 2010 Judi Mason

For further information please contact:
Judi Mason by visiting www.judimason.com
or write to the office of Judi Mason

P.O. Box 7394
Atlanta, GA 30357
Email: info@judimason.com

Layout & Design: Susan L. Volkert
Editing: Akia Walton/Make It Plain Editing & Scott Roberts
Published by: DIVA Ink

Library of Congress Control Number: 2010937891
Printed in the United States of America
ISBN: 978-0-615-40437-0

All rights are reserved. No part of this publication may be reproduced or transmitted in any form or by any means, electronic or mechanical, including photocopying, recording or by any information storage and retrieval system, without the prior written permission of the author, except for the inclusion of brief quotations in a review.

Contents

Acknowledgments, vii

Preface, ix

Letter From The Author, xii

Chapter 1 – Hi, My Name Is Chloe, 1

Chapter 2 – Forgiveness, 7

Chapter 3 – What Is Your Focus?, 13

Chapter 4 – Enjoy Life, 19

Chapter 5 – Sitting In Your Mess, 25

Chapter 6 – Show Your Appreciation, 31

Chapter 7 – I Am Your Special Gift, 37

Chapter 8 – Conflict Resolution, 43

Chapter 9 – Encourage Yourself, 49

Chapter 10 – Fix Your Face, 55

Chapter 11 – Poop-A-Scoop, 61

Chapter 12 – Retreat, 67

Chapter 13 – Chloe Mantra, 73

Epilogue, 77

Acknowledgments

I would like to thank those who worked so diligently to help this book become a reality:

Sheeri Mitchell: Thank you for helping me find my voice as a writer. Your encouragement and editing have been a major contribution to my success. Thank you!

Kim Sheffield: THANK YOU for bringing this book to life. You took my vision and made it come alive. Words can't begin to express my gratitude.

Akia Walton: You are my 25th-hour editing angel. Thank you!

Preface

I would like to thank everyone who painfully pointed out how much Chloe, my cocker spaniel, mimicked my mannerisms during her temper tantrums, mood swings, her charming flirtiness, and snootiness. As much as I did not want to acknowledge it, yes, you were right; she is a lot like me, UGH.

Little did I know that God would use my adorable little baby to force me to take a long, hard look at my attitudes and my actions. It is often impossible for us to see ourselves as others see us until we look in the mirror of our actions, a place where our true reflection is revealed.

When you have a 25-pound "mini me" staring you in the face on a daily basis, you have no choice but to re-examine yourself. In the Bible, God used a donkey to correct a prophet (Numbers 22:28). Well, at least I have a loveable, adorable cocker spaniel. That is better than a donkey any day. I like my odds.

I hope you enjoy reading this first installment of *The Chronicle* book series as much as I enjoyed writing it.

Letter From The Author

When my six-week-old cocker spaniel Chloe arrived, I had mixed emotions. She was an adorable ball of fur and I was truly enamored with her, but she came during a "high stress" period in my life. I was very selfish and self-centered. The only thing that I was concerned about was me. I did not have any restrictions in life. I was single and I lived alone and could come and go as I pleased. But with the addition of Chloe came responsibilities. One responsibility that I hate in particular is house cleaning. I could no longer leave items lying around because they would soon become her chew toys. My every decision from that moment was affected by another living creature. The bottom line was this: I had to grow up.

My after-work excursions to the mall, dinners with friends, impromptu errands, etc., all ended abruptly because Chloe needed to be fed, walked, and loved. There was never a time that I resented Chloe. Initially, however, there was resistance to change on both ends. I really did not feel like taking the time to give her the attention she needed and deserved. But Ms. Chloe was determined to live life with me on her own terms, which meant she *would* get the time and attention she needed and deserved.

If Chloe was mad at me, she made sure that I knew it. I punished her by sending her to her kennel, but that was no punishment at all, it was a joy. In those first few months she loved the kennel because it kept her away from me. When she was really angry, Chloe would defy me by using my bed as a bathroom and destroying select items of clothing (usually the most expensive ones). Our relationship deteriorated into a battle of wills. The problem we both faced was that we had each met our match in the other. At one point, the constant conflict became so unbearable that I gave her away. Our parting lasted for two days. I was miserable without my Chloe. I think she felt the same. Both humbled by our "separation," we gave living together another try. After many months of compromise and adjustments on both ends, we fell in love with each other.

Five years later, Chloe and I understand each other better than we ever have. It's amazing the things and events that God will use to teach you about yourself. And daily that is where I have found myself. In the midst of watching, teaching, or disciplining Chloe, the Lord was simultaneously doing the same to me. It was as if I were looking in a mirror at a four-legged version of myself. What an ego booster! At least she is cute, which is a plus.

This book is my attempt to share those lessons that God taught me through my "parenting" Chloe. I hope the following "snapshots" from my life with Chloe bring you joy and laughter. But more importantly, I hope they afford you the opportunity to be transformed into a better and more complete you, as they did for me. To that end, at the close of each chapter I have provided "challenges, lessons, and nuggets" which are designed to encourage you to apply, learn from, and think about (respectively) the principles introduced in that chapter.

Who knew that a dog could teach you how to love and live a better life? At least she is cheaper than therapy…then again, maybe not.

Enjoy,
Judi & Chloe

Chapter 1
Hi, My Name Is Chloe

*T*HERE ARE VERY FEW TIMES in your life that something so wonderful comes along that you must truly stop to celebrate and honor it.

Six years ago, a couple of male friends and I agreed that we wanted a pet. We never really discussed the matter. It was just understood that we were getting a dog. The two friends were roommates so the logistics of ownership were simple. We agreed that we would share custody of our pooch and I would be the standby auntie.

One day another friend called and told me about a woman giving away cocker spaniel puppies. Well, that was it; I took off. An hour later, I was the proud auntie to a precious cocker named Emma. After taking a good long look at her, I decided that "Chloe" was a better fit. So Emma became Chloe.

Chloe's two dads and I had initially decided we would alternate weeks with her; some weeks she would stay with me and others with them. When those two grown men took their first look at Chloe, they were hooked. They were in love. Chloe had them at HELLO! Having formed an instant bond, they took her from my house and quite literally rolled off into the sunset. It seemed the perfect start to a beautiful friendship. But it was a lie.

Before my custodial weekend rolled around, Chloe was evicted. As it turned out, when her dads left for work, they left her in a fenced-off area in the kitchen. This set-up did not work for Chloe so she figured out a way to escape and search for her daddies. At that point, she did what most puppies do; she gnawed, chewed and scratched at a closed door trying to gain access. Shortly after the honeymoon began, I knew it was over when I received an irate phone call which consisted of only five words: "She has got to go." At that moment, the tables turned. I became Mom and my two friends became Chloe's uncles.

As far as I was concerned, the transition would be seamless. I forged ahead with all the optimism and confidence of a new doggie-parent full of "I can do all things" enthusiasm. I didn't stand a chance. As the custodial parent, I was in for a treat. The first few months were rough, to say the least. Chloe, who came to be known as "the little diva," did not understand that there can be only one Diva (with a capital "D"), and that *she* is *me*. So, the battle of the wills began. The battle would morph into a long, difficult war. But in the end, we both surrendered and fell in love with each other.

The love I have for Chloe is indescribable. She is such a loving and affectionate dog. She invites you to love on her, but lavishly loves on you as well. She always seems genuinely happy to see you. Her love is truly unconditional; unless treats are involved, and at that point, she is shamelessly partial.

Little did I know that this bundle of love and joy that I had been given a second chance with was there to teach me a few lessons. It was all a set-up. Trust me when I say that God has a sense of humor.

Nugget:

*God can and will use anything,
yes, anything to show you yourself.
Allow yourself the opportunity to open up to
receive and learn some of the simple lessons that
are right before you.
I believe they will be life changing.*

Notes

Chapter 2
Forgiveness

*T*HERE IS NOTHING MORE HUMBLING than when someone who has committed an offense against you comes in a spirit of humility, fear, and meekness seeking forgiveness. If you have even a small amount of compassion, you have no choice but to forgive. Now imagine a 10-month-old adorable puppy coming to you with head held down, walking approximately a step an hour, seeking forgiveness for chewing my clothes, pooping on the floor, being defiant, running in the street, eating my Famous Amos chocolate chip cookies (that one took a minute to forgive), jumping on unauthorized furniture and did I mention eating my Famous Amos chocolate chip cookies?

There are so many situations where Chloe tested my patience and I am sure I have tested hers as well. Throughout our many conflicts, Chloe unwittingly taught me numerous lessons on forgiveness. She showed me how to forgive and how to be forgiven. For example, there were times when Chloe indicated her desire to play or go for a walk and I put that "request" on hold to meet a deadline, complete a project, take a phone call, or give my attention to any number of important things. Instead of sulking, she politely waited her turn. I am sure she was disappointed but she never showed it. When I finally finished my task, she was just as enthusiastic as she was when she made her initial request. All disappointment at having to wait on me was forgotten. If I am to be completely honest, I don't know if I would be so understanding if the shoe were on the other foot. Depending on the situation, I might be a bit put off for having to wait; freely displaying my attitude for the individual to see and letting them know, in no uncertain terms, how I felt. I might even refuse to play or participate... yep, I know, real mature. But by her actions, Chloe has taught me not to hold grudges but to communicate my needs and wants.

Forgiveness means that I have to release my right to be angry, disappointed, frustrated, and otherwise offended. It took me a while to fully understand, comprehend, and apply that principle to my life. But I have come a long way with the help of my furry friend, and I can say that I am better for it.

Challenge:

Take a moment to consider your life.
Is there anyone that you need to forgive today?
Do you need to be forgiven?
Do you need to forgive yourself?
If so, do it now.

Release the hurt, pain, and frustration that hindered you because of your unwillingness to forgive and embrace love, joy, and freedom.
The first step is deciding that you want to be free.
If you are overwhelmed by the pain, just take it one day at a time.
Release a bit of it each day, and pretty soon, the pain will be gone.
I promise you God will meet you where you are and walk you through the rest.

Notes

Chapter 3
What Is Your Focus?

*T*HERE IS NEVER A TIME that I am eating that Chloe doesn't make it her business to sit on the periphery of her prohibited area and gaze longingly at my food. She sits in silence tilting her head from one side to the other, silently begging with her eyes for a morsel or two. She waits in quiet anticipation, longing and hoping that I will share my meal.

I believe that she knows that she will eventually stare me down long enough and I will give in. And she is right, I often do. During these episodes where my food is the sole object of her focused attention, I find it surprising how she often fails to realize that I have already dropped pieces of it on the floor. So focused on my eating that she misses the very thing for which she is actively begging. Her single-minded tunnel vision blinds her to the treats that I have quite literally laid at her feet.

One day, while observing this behavior, I had an epiphany: We are no different than Chloe. We are so busy looking for the bigger picture, that we miss the small stills that help make it a reality. How many blessings have you been blinded to because you had the wrong focus? Sometimes, the thing that you are longing for the most can be right in front of you. But you will miss it if your focus is off, even a little. Chloe appears to be looking in the right direction—even at the right thing—but she still misses her blessing. Do you?

Ask yourself:

❖ Where is your focus?

❖ Who or what are you looking at that could be causing you to miss what is right in front of you?

❖ On what or who are you so fixated on that you have missed the blessing that God has set apart just for you?

❖ What are you looking for or longing for so badly that you can't conceive that there may be an alternative?

Take time today to re-examine your focus. Acknowledge the blinders of distraction and deception that have been put over your eyes. Make the choice to remove those blinders in order to see your life and circumstances with clarity.

I had to learn to stop looking for instant gratification and teach myself to appreciate the small blessings. They are just as important as the bigger ones. More often than not, you will find that they are even bigger because without them, you are unable to make it to your final goal or destination.

How much have you missed by focusing on the wrong thing?

Nugget:

Sometimes we stare so long at a door that is closing that we see too late the one that is open.

~ Alexander Graham Bell ~

Notes

Chapter 4
Enjoy Life

I HAVE NEVER SEEN A DOG AS LOVING as Chloe. She greets every creature as if to say, "Hello!" She shamelessly encourages a pet or coo from people and a sniff in very inappropriate places from her counterparts.

One day in the park, a fellow walker commented that Chloe was such a happy dog. At that moment, I realized what joy Chloe brings to others with her carefree, fun-loving nature. Joggers, walkers, and dogs alike pause to take notice. It is as if those she encounters recognizes a smile on her face. She brings happiness to everyone that she comes across. Her joy is truly contagious.

We would do well to take a page from Chloe's book. She truly knows how to live and enjoy life. How great would it be if humans were as carefree and loving as animals? In spite of the responsibilities and challenges of life, we need to allow ourselves the freedom and opportunity to live and enjoy life intentionally in order to experience the true joys that life really has to offer.

Challenge:

Take time daily to remove yourself from the rat race of life and allow yourself the privilege to experience moments of true bliss! Purposefully seek out things and people that bring you joy. And you will see how liberated you will become. Be sure to pay it forward and share your new found joy and contentment with others.

Notes

Chapter 5
Sitting In Your Mess

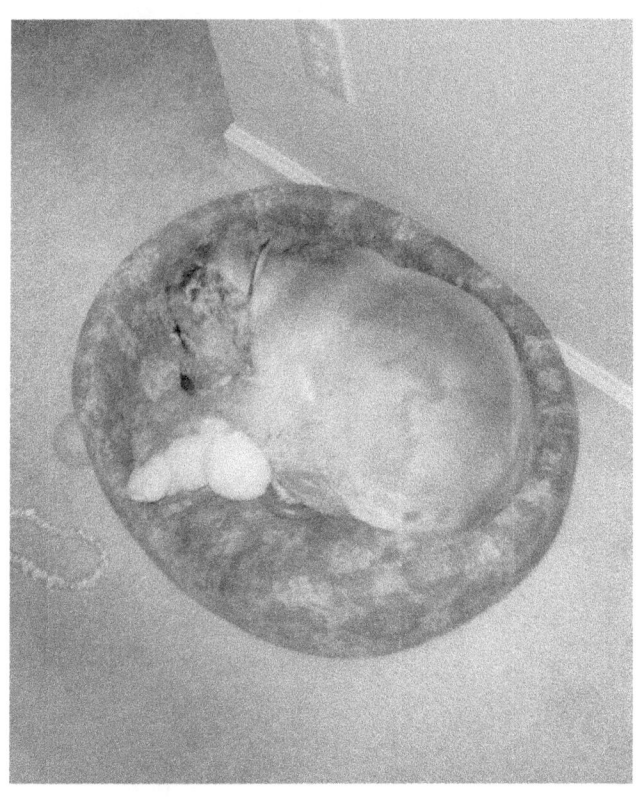

$\mathcal{O}$NE MORNING I WOKE UP to a stench like no other. Chloe had pooped on my bed. Apparently she did not feel well and what she might have mistaken for gas was something else. Thank God it was only on my comforter and not on me. As I began to get up to clean up the mess, I realized that I was looking at my life.

At the time I had so many challenges, from financial to relational and everything in between, that waking up surrounded by poop was a harsh reality check. I was so overwhelmed trying to figure out how to handle all of my problems that it seemed like every time I thought I had a handle on one situation, the next problem was substantially worst. As I began cleaning up the mess that surrounded me, I noticed the pattern in which I was cleaning, layer by layer—first the comforter, then the sheets, then the mattress. During this process I realized this is the exact method that I needed to use to handle my problems. I needed to deal with each issue one at a time.

I know this isn't rocket science, but I believe that my mind was so bombarded with everything going on that instead of being proactive, I was being reactive. In doing so, I grappled for quick fixes and easy solutions to ease the pain. What I really needed to do was to step back, take control, strategize, prioritize, and handle one issue at a time. This method would allow me the ability to be more productive, be less stressed, and realize a more successful outcome.

Lesson:

*If you are confronted with overwhelming issues,
don't tackle them all at once.
Just take it one issue at a time.
It will help you gain control over your situation
and most of all, your sanity.*

Notes

Chapter 6
Show Your Appreciation

How IS IT that someone who doesn't work, pay bills, clean up the house, or even cook can demand so much attention or need so much personal space? Did I mention that she doesn't work or pay bills? Prime example: If I am in my bedroom on my bed (notice, MY bed) and I am on the phone, Chloe has to jump off the bed or has to remove herself from the immediate area because I am disturbing her. I am sorry, DISTURBING HER!!!! How can I disturb you? You don't have a job! I neglected to mention that as she removes herself from the general area, she looks at me and rolls her eyes with MAJOR attitude. Once again, I state, YOU DON'T HAVE A JOB!!!!!!

When I am working in my home office on the computer or making calls, I will receive a wet nose nudge indicating either play time or I NEED ATTENTION. And if I don't respond or move in a timely manner, I will be nudged repeatedly, until I either give a command or give in. Lord, where did she come from?

In Chloe's mind, it is all about her wants and needs. Her selfish actions made me realize how selfish and self-centered I had become with those that I love. So much so, that I felt compelled to call each of my loved ones to confess my selfishness, and to express my profound gratitude for their love and friendship. This experience brought us closer and prompted me to be more aware of my expectations and my actions toward others. Surprisingly, making those calls turned out to be the most liberating experience. It fostered new depths of communication and facilitated new levels of growth in my relationships.

My heart's desire is that you, too, would experience such a life-changing encounter. It will enrich your relationships to a deeper level. At one time or another all of us have taken a loved one or a dear friend for granted. Usually the person you love and depend on the most is the very one you neglect.

Challenge:

*The title says it all! Do not pass go on this one.
Pick up the phone, and call your parents,
siblings, and/or friends.
Express your love and gratitude and
apologize (if need be) for taking them for granted.
Show them the appreciation that they deserve.
They will be glad you did.*

Notes

Chapter 7
I Am Your Special Gift

*C*HLOE IS A FIRM BELIEVER in spreading the love. As much as she loves to give it, she also loves to receive it. It doesn't matter if you're a neighbor she sees daily, or a stranger simply walking down the street. In Chloe's mind it is the duty of every human being to pet her, coo at her, adore her, and love on her. Likewise it is every dog's responsibility to play with her. The hardest thing to witness is when Chloe is rejected by a person or another animal. The hurt and disappointment on her face is disheartening. The bright side is that her moments of rejection last for approximately three seconds (if that long). Either something else catches her attention and she runs along after it, or another friendlier human being or animal will happen by.

As far as rejection is concerned, Chloe does better than most humans. She is very forgiving. She knows how to let things go and move on. When rejected, she turns away, but will sometimes turn back as if to offer the transgressor one more opportunity to reconsider. If the rejection occurs again, she will go about her merry way unaffected. Surprisingly, if she encounters the same person or animal in the same day, week, or month, she will approach them as if the previous incident never occurred. It is amazing what she chooses to retain and what she chooses to let go. I have learned by Chloe's actions that some things are not worth my time, emotions, or attention. This lesson has really helped me to stay focused on the important things in life and to ignore the distractions.

Lesson:

Do you need to start letting go of things that are not worth your time or energy?
If someone rejects you, take your cue from Chloe, ignore them. Don't get offended.
Don't give them space in your mind; keep it moving.
If you encounter them again, walk in that same love.
If they reject you again, shrug it off.
Obviously, they don't realize the valuable gift that you are.

Chloe's attitude is that everyone who meets her is better off for having been in her presence.
You and I should feel the same.
You are of value. You are a gift. You are of worth.
Now share that gift with the ones who are wise enough to recognize and respect it.

Notes

Chapter 8
Conflict Resolution

When it comes to arguments, Chloe has taught me the valuable lesson of "agreeing to disagree." Chloe has no problem putting herself in time out, especially on days when she has been overzealous with the trash, clothing, or paper products. When caught in the act, she definitely knows how to run the other way. However when she is ready to make up, she employs her own method.

Once Chloe has committed her transgression and endured her self-appointed time out, her conflict resolution begins. When the proverbial smoke has cleared, she begins to survey the land. She creeps around the house, sniffing me out. Once she locates me, she enters the room and occupies the corner farthest from me and quietly watches me as if to discern my temperament. Most of the time, I am oblivious to her presence. When she senses that the atmosphere is conducive for an approach, she makes one. At that time, I will discuss the error of her ways. Without fail, she humbly listens with her head hung low. Once I complete my lecture, as a sign of an apology, she will either lick my face or nudge her nose against my leg. In response, I will usually speak affectionately to her or pet her head. Taking this as a sign of my forgiveness, Chloe bolts for her toys; I can only assume that play time means life is good in her world.

These interactions with Chloe illustrated for me how to handle disagreements. Her seeking me out forces me to grow up and face head on the issue that divides us. It has taken some time for me to apply these principles in my own life. But instead of avoiding an uncomfortable issue, nursing hurt feelings, or glossing over a disagreement, like I normally would, I confront it. This new phase in my life has really caused some growing pains. But in the long run it has made my relationships healthier and stronger.

How do you handle disagreements? Once it is all said and done, do you discuss the issue(s) and rectify the problem(s), or do you "move on" in anger and bitterness? Do you acknowledge your part in the situation, or do you just point and blame before sitting in a corner to pout?

Challenge:

The next time a conflict arises try
Chloe's Conflict Resolution:

Put yourself in time out.

Allow both parties time to cool off.

Assess the part that you played in the matter.

Attempt to see the situation from
the other party's point of view.

Once you are ready to talk, survey the land.
Check the temperament of the other parties involved.

Deal with the situation accordingly.
Confront the issues at hand.

Some issues can be resolved immediately
and some take time.
At least be proactive in dealing with the situation.

Once it is all said and done,
make amends and celebrate.

Notes

Chapter 9
Encourage Yourself

(Chloe admiring her reflection)

I LOVE THE POETRY AND SYMMETRY in the Bible. In the book of Psalms, King David wrote that he was fearfully and wonderfully made. (Psalms 139:13-14) I often wonder if he had Chloe in mind when he wrote that Psalm. I have never seen a dog that gazes at herself in the mirror with such admiration. The sight of her preening truly amazes me. As her owner, I believe I have the right to say that Chloe is an adorable dog. However, it appears that Chloe is also aware of this fact and would probably dare you to tell her differently. Even on her worst days, she seems confident in her beauty.

Have you ever had one of those days in which you felt like you were invincible, only to discover later that your hair was standing on the top of your head, your pants zipper was down, or that (when you dressed in the dark) you'd put your shirt on inside out? I know it's hard to believe, but so has Chloe. There have been times when she has left the groomer and upon seeing her, I shrank back in horror wondering, "What did they do to my little baby?" At those times, Chloe has looked like the dog from the movie *My Dog Skip*, on crack.

On more than one occasion, I have found myself fervently praying for her hair to grow back INSTANTLY! Unfortunately that prayer has never been answered. Instead, I had to endure the pleasure of showcasing a dog whose fur appeared to have lost a fight with a pair of very angry clippers. Needless to say, it was at those very times that Chloe would strut and prance around like a contestant in a beauty pageant, oblivious to her hideous appearance.

I remain utterly convinced that even if she knew how awful she looked, my overly confident cocker spaniel would still prance and strut. This brings me to my point. No matter how bad your day is going or how low your confidence or self esteem may be at any given point, remember you are fearfully and wonderfully made. You are invincible and you can do it. Just encourage yourself. You are your best cheerleader.

Nugget:

If you are having one of those days and you need a little motivation, just think of Chloe looking like a skinned cat, strutting down the sidewalk like a Parisian model on a runway. If she can do that, you can do anything.

Now go show the world what you have to offer— even if your shirt is on backwards.

Notes

Chapter 10
Fix Your Face

It's written all over your face, you don't have to say a word...

THERE ARE TIMES when I tell Chloe to do something, such as go sit down or go outside. And sometimes she will look at me as if to say, "*You are the biggest idiot.*" Her upper lip will lift and tuck to expose portions of her teeth. She reminds me of Elvis when he raised his upper lip during a performance. On these occasions, I politely let her know to "fix your face." I have no idea where the saying came from, but one day I just opened my mouth and said it and instantly, she understood. Once that command is given, she cautiously drops her head, adjusts her attitude, and finds a quiet place to reflect.

I believe that God gave me that saying not for Chloe but for me. So often in life, when I need a severe attitude adjustment, I find myself needing to fix my face. However I don't perform my face transformation with Chloe's humility. When I encounter upsetting situations, I go from one ludicrous extreme to the other. In the end, I only wind up hurting myself.

Each day, I am learning to FIX MY FACE, to behave like a big girl and deal patiently with whatever or whomever distresses me. Hopefully one day, I will be able to manage my facial transformation with the same ease Chloe seems to have mastered. We can only hope!

Lesson:

There are days when you find yourself in desperate
need of an attitude adjustment.
On those days, instead of reacting like you
normally would, take a moment,
gather your thoughts, and FIX YOUR FACE.

I have witnessed in my own life how much drama
I have avoided by performing a minor face adjustment.
It really helps avoid a lot of unnecessary problems, frustration,
and pain.

Notes

Chapter 11
Poop-A-Scoop

Please note this offering is not meant to be offensive, gross, or graphic. It is simply an effective word picture that perfectly conveys my point. Please bear with me.

*H*AVE YOU EVER HAD TO poop-a-scoop? For all of you non-dog owners, poop-a-scoop is when you have to scoop your pooch's poop from the lawn. Well, I am here to tell you, it is the most humbling experience to have to scoop someone else's poop. The more often I perform this procedure, the more I begin to notice how the digestive system works. It is evident that some food is digested and completely processed, while other food passes through whole. I find it amazing that the body instinctively knows what to purge and how to purge it. Chloe's system is of such a sensitive nature that if she eats foods foreign to her body, it will pass within thirty minutes to an hour. However, if she eats something that her body is familiar with, digestion requires a little more time. But even then, some things are fully processed, while other things remain whole.

Unlike Chloe's digestive system, most people's emotional processing system operates poorly when it comes to processing the adversities that come our way. There are so many turbulent situations and circumstances that we hold onto because we do not know how to let them go. We don't know how to label them or how to relinquish them into the proper trash receptacles of life. Just as Chloe's body does not allow foreign items to accumulate or remain in her system, we should not allow negativity and emotional toxic waste to accumulate in ours. We need to form an emotional pooper scooper that removes all toxins—so that anything which prevents healthy emotional development is eliminated and not digested. Our hearts need to become a place where only those experiences which foster love, joy, peace, harmony, and unity remain, leaving us with peace of mind, soul, and spirit.

Challenge:

Take a good look at your life. Do you have toxins: negativity and/or dead weight holding you down? Do you need to replace some things in your life with peace, tranquility, and fulfillment? Vow that you will reject negativity! Allow it to stay where it is—in the giver's hand, mouth, mind, or heart. It has no place in your life. Take time to poop-a-scoop your life and set yourself free!

Notes

Chapter 12
Retreat

*C*HLOE IS SUCH THE SOCIALITE that naturally when another dog barks outside or a doggie convention convenes on the sidewalk, she wants to participate. When she can't go directly to the action, she settles for the balcony. From her vantage point three stories high, she can observe all the neighborhood happenings and offer an occasional bark.

Recently, however, the balcony has taken on a different function in Chloe's daily routine. Instead of using it to gain access to neighborhood gossip, she has begun to use it as a place to retreat. I started to notice that Chloe would lounge on the balcony to enjoy a cool breeze, check out the neighborhood happenings, commune with nature, and even take a mid-afternoon nap. What she once used for social interaction turned into a place of tranquility.

Chloe's social haven now serves double-duty as her sanctuary. Each day, she spends multiple 15-30 minute intervals on the balcony (depending on the weather) just to take a break from the routines of life. So often we get caught up in the day-to-day activities that we neglect to take the time to relax and enjoy the moment. By her example, Chloe showed a workaholic like me how to take a moment for myself to rejuvenate my mind, body, and spirit. I learned how to turn an ordinary place into a sanctuary.

Lesson:

Do you find yourself in need of a retreat?
Do you have a place at home or work where
you can escape?
If not, take time to create one.
If so, make that place special by adding personal
effects such as a candle, potpourri, or something
that makes it feel more peaceful.
Enjoy your private haven as often as possible—
daily if you can manage it.
Doing so will keep you grounded, focused, energized,
and most of all, peaceful.
We all need to take a tranquil break from time to time.
Go ahead; treat yourself.
You've earned it.

Notes

Chapter 13
Chloe Mantra:
Live, Love & Enjoy Life

CHLOE HAS TAUGHT ME how to live, love, and just enjoy life through the following lessons:

- Love unconditionally!
- Forgive immediately!
- Attempt to rectify an error or mistake instantly.
- Let go of an offense: IT'S NOT WORTH IT!!!!
- Play with those who want to play with you. Walk away from those who don't.
- Realize you can't force anyone to like or love you. If they are unable to see your worth, then they are obviously not worthy of you.
- Believe you are special! You are valuable! You are worthy! Accept it! Embrace it! Walk in it!
- Most of all, know that you are loved.
- Sow love and you will reap love.

Notes

Epilogue

On April 28, 2009, I lost my best friend Chloe to kidney disease. At the tender age of five, she had done more for me than most people that I have known. The love that she showed and the patience she possessed helped me to become a better person. She touched everyone she came in contact with and her infectious personality made every day bright. She taught me to live life to the fullest because that is truly what she did. It was a privilege to care for and learn from such an extraordinary animal. She was truly special and will continue to be missed.

This book is a celebration of her life and her legacy of love.

I believe the love and patience that Chloe showed me is an example of the love that is displayed in the Bible. As a Christian, I've found that the greatest love of all is that of Jesus Christ. If you are interested in finding out more information about the unconditional love of Jesus Christ or the Christian faith, feel free to visit: www.judimason.com/faith

Thank you for allowing me to share Chloe with you.
Be sure to share yourself with others, live on purpose,
and enjoy life. Chloe did and I know I will too.

Thanks so much for your support. I hope you have enjoyed *The Chloe Chronicles*, the first installment of the three-part *Chronicle* series, which also includes *The Relationship Chronicles: Straight Talk…Real Love…No Drama!* and *The Best Self Chronicles: Discovering Your Authentic Self.* The second and third parts are due out summer 2012.

Be sure to pick up your copies!

Let's stay connected:

Be sure to visit my blog and add your name to my email list to stay abreast of the latest happenings. Just sign up on my website: www.judimason.com

Follow Me on...

Twitter: twitter.com/judimason

Facebook: facebook.com/judimason.empowerment

Have a question? Email me at: judi@divaink.com

From my heart:

I really want you to become the BEST YOU that you can be. Make every day count and choose to live on purpose.
Let's make YOUR DREAMS become a reality!

Much love,

Judi

Empowered to empower others!

www.ingramcontent.com/pod-product-compliance
Lightning Source LLC
LaVergne TN
LVHW011427080426
835512LV00005B/319